Building Word #2

MW01273187

Grades 1-2

Written by Margot Southall
Illustrated by S&S Learning Materials Ltd.

ISBN 1-55035-350-0
Copyright 1995
Revised October 2006
All Rights Reserved * Printed in Canada

Published in the United States by:
On The Mark Press
3909 Witmer Road PMB 175
Niagara Falls, New York
14305
www.onthemarkpress.com

Published in Canada by:
S&S Learning Materials
15 Dairy Avenue
Napanee, Ontario
K7R 1M4
www.sslearning.com

Look For
Other Language Units

Building Word Families #2

Table of Contents

Building Word Families #2

Organization of the Program

1. The word building activities in this unit are designed to be used for working with small groups or individual students. The step by step procedures are easily mastered by tutors or parent volunteers.

2. Phonics rules are provided in the following pages to assist in planning a logical sequence of lessons and activities.

3. You may wish to use these activities as part of your regular reading group program, alternating word building with guided and independent reading.

4. With your class, brainstorm lists of words for each of the Short and Long Vowel Word Families, Consonant Blends and Digraphs and record them on a chart. Use the Word Family Labels at the top of each list as a pictorial aid. You may also wish to focus on the vowel digraphs and dipthongs included in this unit, using the word family as a springboard to discuss and list other words using these spelling patterns.

5. Student instructions for matching the word puzzles are on the word building mat accompanying this unit. However, it is suggested that the teacher model at the beginning of the program each important step including the voicing of the phonogram, initial consonant, consonant blend or digraph as well as each new word.

6. Store each word family activity in a labeled ziploc bag or envelope and list the consonants, blends or digraphs that should be included. The manipulative sheet may be used for this.

7. Photocopy the manipulatives onto brightly colored paper (available at office supply stores), then mount and laminate in the usual way or have students or volunteers color the illustrations.

Building Word Families #2

8. To make the slide card manipulative, follow the directions on the sheet provided using the following diagram as a guide:

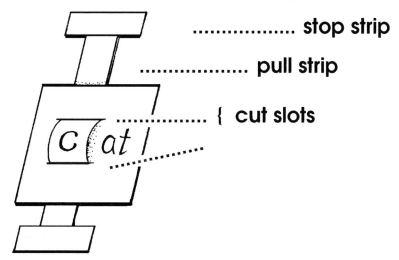

.... **stop strip**

.... **pull strip**

.... { **cut slots**

9. Additional word recognition activities may be created by programming and duplicating the Word Card Form for students to sort into labeled "mailboxes" or "pockets".

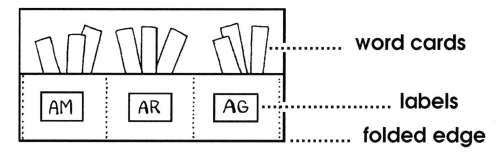

.... **word cards**

.... **labels**

.... **folded edge**

10. The Word Cards may also be used for games such as "Happy Families", "Snap", "Concentration" and "Go Fish" as a fun way for students to reinforce their recognition of the phonograms taught.

11. The review sheets are designed to be used after the introduction of every two or three word families. These may be used as a whole group activity.

12. To assist students experiencing difficulty in the visual recognition and auditory blending of words, use magnetic letters on a slate or blackboard before introducing students to the puzzles and slide cards. Have the students match the initial consonant, blend or digraph to the word by sliding it in place using the Teacher - Student Prompts as a guide.

Building Word Families #2

Teacher - Student Prompts

The following teacher guide is meant to be used with individual or small group word building sessions and may be mounted on tag board and laminated for classroom use.

1. Focus on the <u>word family</u> represented on the slide card or puzzle piece. Say:

   "What <u>letters</u> make the _____ (word family) sound?"

   "What <u>sound</u> does ____ (letters) make?"

   Encourage the student to blend the letters so that they sound right.

2. Focus on the initial consonant, consonant blend or digraph on the slide or puzzle piece. Say:

   "What <u>letter</u> is this?"

   "What <u>sound</u> does ___ (letter) make?"

3. Ask the student to place both the puzzle pieces side by side. If using a slide card, model how it works. Say:

   "Make me a <u>word</u> with the _____ (word family) sound."

   "What <u>word</u> have you made?"

   Ask the student to run a finger underneath the word to assist him/her to sequence the letters/sounds correctly.

   Say:

   "Can you say it <u>slowly</u>?"

   "Can you say it <u>fast</u>?"

Building Word Families #2

4. To review, say:

   "In the word (the student has made) what <u>letters</u> make the _____ (word family) sound?"

   "What <u>sound</u> does _____ (letters in the word family) make?"

   "What <u>letter</u> makes the _____ (initial consonat, blend or digraph) sound?"

   "What <u>sound</u> does _____ (letter) make?"

   "What is the whole word?"

   Have the student print the word on the recording sheet using the manipulative as a guide.

5. To build the remaining words, have the student put the next beginning letter/s in place and then ask him or her to say the previous (familiar) word, then to repeat it, but substituting the new initial consonant, blend or digraph. For example:

   "Say the word "bake". Now say the word again but instead of "b" say "m"."

6. You may wish to continue further by asking the student:

   "Can you write me the word _____ (one of the words that he or she has built)?"

   Continue for each of the words. You may wish to use a chalkboard or have the student use colored markers for this exercise.

Building Word Families #2

Phonics Overview

The following phonics principles are incorporated into the activities in this unit:

Single Vowel Letters

The vowel letters are used to record a vowel sound. The vowel letters are _a_, _e_, _i_, _o_, _u_ and sometimes _y_. All the other letters in the alphabet are consonants. For example:

- _a_ as in _at_
- _e_ as in _egg_
- _i_ as in _it_
- _o_ as in _ox_
- _u_ as in _up_

Long Vowel Sounds

The five long vowel sounds are articulated the same as their letter names:

- _a_\\ as in _cake_
- _e_\\ as in _feet_
- _i_\\ as in _nice_
- _o_\\ as in _coat_
- _u_\\ as in _blue_

The long vowel sounds occur in the initial, medial and final positions of words or syllables.

The long \\u\\ sound is a combination of the consonant \\y\\ and the vowel sound \\u\\. The long \\u\\ sounds are \\yoo\\ heard in new and the \\oo\\ sound heard in blue. These sounds can be spelled _u__e_, _ue_ or _ew_.

Building Word Families #2

Short Vowel Sounds

The five short vowel sounds are:

- \$\backslash a \backslash$\ as in _cat_
- \$\backslash e \backslash$\ as in _get_
- \$\backslash i \backslash$\ as in _bit_
- \$\backslash a \backslash$\ as in _hot_
- \$\backslash u \backslash$\ as in _nut_

The short vowel sounds occur in initial and medial positions in words or syllables, but seldom in the final position.

The short "u" sound is often referred to as the schwa sound, which is written as an inside down e.

The short sound of \e\ can be spelled three ways. For example: _set_, _head_, _said_.

Teaching Tip: Have students practice forming their mouths correctly to make each vowel sound. A mirror is useful in tutoring sessions.

Dipthongs

A vowel dipthong is voiced by moving from one vowel position to another within a single enunciation. For example:

- _oi_\ as in _noise_
- _oy_\ as in _toy_
- _au_\ as in _haunt_
- _aw_\ as in _saw_
- _ou_\ as in _house_
- _ow_\ as in _cow_

The sound \oi\ can be spelled as \oy\ or \oi\ as in _toy_ and _coin_. The \ou\ sound can be spelled \ow\ or \ou\ as in _how_ and _sound_.

Building Word Families #2

Consonant Blends

The term *consonant blends* refers to sounds rather than letters. A consonant blend is a combination of two or more consonant sounds occurring together in the initial or final position in a syllable or word. For example *blue* and *fast*.

Blends with "r"

- *br*\ as in *brown*
- *cr*\ as in *cry*
- *dr*\ as in *drum*
- *fr*\ as in *frog*
- *gr*\ as in *green*
- *pr*\ as in *present*
- *tr*\ as in *try*

Blends with "l"

- *bl*\ as in *blue*
- *cl*\ as in *class*
- *fl*\ as in *fly*
- *gl*\ as in *glad*
- *pl*\ as in *play*
- *sl*\ as in *sled*

Blend with "s"

- *sk*\ as in *skin*
- *sm*\ as in *small*
- *sn*\ as in *snow*
- *sp*\ as in *spot*
- *st*\ as in *stop*
- *sw*\ as in *sweet*

Building Word Families #2

Consonant Digraphs

A consonant digraph represents one sound with two consonant letters. The following consonant digraphs included in this unit occur in the initial positions of syllables.

- _ch_\ as in _chair_
- _sh_\ as in _ship_
- _th_\ as in _thin_
- _wh_\ as in _why_

Three of these digraphs can also occur in the final position in syllables.

- _ch_\ as in _lunch_
- _sh_\ as in _fish_
- _th_\ as in _with_

Phonics Rules

The following phonics generalizations may be of help to young readers:

1. A vowel is usually short if it comes between two consonants. This can be represented as (C+)VC where C represents a consonant, V a vowel and + means that more than one letter may occur. For example: _cat_, _pet_, _kit_, _hot_, _cub_.

   Teaching Tip: Encourage students to try a short vowel sound when attempting to read a word with this pattern. Remind students that a word must make sense, sound right and look right.

2. In words with a C(+)V pattern try a long vowel sound. For example: _we_, _go_. The exceptions are _do_ and _to_.

3. In words with a (C+)VCe pattern try a long vowel sound. For example: _cap_ - _cape_, _pet_ - _Pete_, _kit_ - _kite_, _hop_ - _hope_, _cut_ - _cute_. This is known as the silent e rule.

Building Word Families #2

4. If the letter "c" is followed by e, i or y, it will usually have a soft \s\ sound and a \g\ will have the soft \j\ sound. For example: _cent_, _city_, _gym_ and _magic_. The exceptions are _get_ and _give_.

5. When two vowels occur side by side the first vowel is voiced, while the second vowel is silent. For example: _e_\ in _seat_, _a_\ in _rain_.

Objectives For The Unit

Students will be able to:

- identify the correct pronunciation of short and long vowel phonograms (word families) using the pictorial representations as an aid.

- appropriately pronounce words formed by adding single consonants, consonant blends and consonant digraphs to the familiar phonogram.

- reinforce the kinesthetic learning of spelling patterns by recording the words that they have made.

- transfer their experience to the recognition of familiar phonograms in words with more than one syllable.

List of Skills

1. Short and Long Vowel Word Families (phonograms)

   - ade, ake, ame, ave, ate, ail, ain, ay, art, ack, ank, all

   - ell, ent, est, ew

   - ice, ide, ine, ind, ight, ill, ing, ick, ink

   - oke, ose, old, ock, ore

   - ue

Building Word Families #2

2. <u>Word Families with Dipthongs</u>

   • aw, ound, ow as in <u>cow</u>

3. <u>Word Families with Vowel Digraphs</u>

   • ail, ain, air, ay,

   • eak, eam, ear, eat, eed, eep, eet

   • oat, ook, ow as in show

4. <u>Consonant Blends and Clusters</u>

   • br, cr, dr, fr, gr, pr, tr

   • bl, cl, fl, gl, pl, sl

   • sk, sm, sn, sp, st, sw

   • scr, str, thr

5. <u>Consonant Digraphs</u>

   • th, wh, sh, ch

Teacher Evaluation Sheet

Topic : _____

Date : _____

Evaluation Marks:

S - Satisfactory

I - Improving

N - Needs Improvement

U - Unsatisfactory

Students' Names

WORD FAMILIES

The [_____ all] Family

Print the [_____ all] words that you made.

1. _____   4. _____
2. _____   5. _____
3. _____   6. _____

Put a * beside your favorite [____ all] word.

Print it in a sentence.

_____

_____

WORD FAMILIES

The [_____ ank] Family

Print the [____ ank] words that you made.

1. _____   4. _____
2. _____   5. _____
3. _____   6. _____

Put a * beside your favorite [_____ ank] word.

Print it in a sentence.

_____

_____

Instructions: Mount on a sturdy backing and laminate. Cut out the puzzle pieces and store them in a labeled envelope. Students will match the word family with the initial consonant, blend or digraph.

all		b	c
f	sm	t	w

ank		b	bl
s	t	th	cr

WORD FAMILIES

The [_____ ack] Family

Print the [___ ack] words that you made.

1. _____   4. _____
2. _____   5. _____
3. _____   6. _____

Put a * beside your favorite [_____ ack] word.
Print it in a sentence.

_____

_____

WORD FAMILIES

The [_____ ade] Family

Print the [___ ade] words that you made.

1. _____   4. _____
2. _____   5. _____
3. _____   6. _____

Put a * beside your favorite [_____ ade] word.
Print it in a sentence.

_____

_____

Instructions: Mount on a sturdy backing and laminate. Cut out the puzzle pieces and store them in a labeled envlope. The students will match the word family with the initial consonant blend or digraph.

ack		b	s
bl	cr	sn	tr

ade		m	f
bl	w	tr	sh

WORD FAMILIES

The | ____ art | Family

Print the | ____ art | words that you made.

1. _____   4._____
2. _____   5._____
3. _____   6._____

Put a * beside your favorite | ____ art | word.

Print it in a sentence.

_____

_____

WORD FAMILIES

The | ____ ate | Family

Print the | ____ ate | words that you made.

1. _____   4. _____
2. _____   5. _____
3. _____   6. _____

Put a * beside your favorite | ____ ate | word.

Print it in a sentence.

_____

_____

art		d	ch
p	sm	t	c

ate		d	h
g	l	pl	cr

WORD FAMILIES

The [_____ ake] Family

Print the [____ ake] words that you made.

1. _____   4. _____
2. _____   5. _____
3. _____   6. _____

Put a * beside your favorite [_____ ake] word.

Print it in a sentence.

_____

_____

WORD FAMILIES

The [_____ ame] Family

Print the [____ ame] words that you made.

1. _____   4. _____
2. _____   5. _____
3. _____   6. _____

Put a * beside your favorite [_____ ame] word.

Print it in a sentence.

_____

_____

Instructions: Mount on a sturdy backing and laminate. Cut out the puzzle pieces and store them in a labeled envelope. The students will match the word family with the initial consonant, blend or digraph.

ake		b	c
br	l	r	t

ame		c	g
n	s	t	bl

WORD FAMILIES

The | ____ail | Family

Print the | ____ail | words that you made.

1. _____ 4. _____
2. _____ 5. _____
3. _____ 6. _____

Put a * beside your favorite | ____ail | word.

Print it in a sentence.

_____

_____

WORD FAMILIES

The | ____ain | Family

Print the | ____ain | words that you made.

1. _____ 4. _____
2. _____ 5. _____
3. _____ 6. _____

Put a * beside your favorite | ____ain | word.

Print it in a sentence.

_____

_____

Instructions: Mount on a sturdy backing and laminate. Cut out the puzzle pieces and store them in a labeled envelope. Students will match the word family with the initial consonant, blend or digraph.

ail		m	n
p	tr	s	t

ain		br	m
pl	tr	p	r

WORD FAMILIES

The | ____air | Family

Print the | ____air | words that you made.

1. _____   4. _____
2. _____   5. _____
3. _____   6. _____

Put a * beside your favorite | ____air | word.
Print it in a sentence.

_____

_____

WORD FAMILIES

The | ____ave | Family

Print the | ____ ave | words that you made.

1. _____   4. _____
2. _____   5. _____
3. _____   6. _____

Put a * beside your favorite | ____ave | word.
Print it in a sentence.

_____

_____

Instructions: Mount on a sturdy backing and laminate. Cut out the puzzle pieces and store them in a labeled envelope. Students will match the word family with the initial consonant, blend or digraph.

air		f	h
ch	p	st	fl

ave		c	br
g	s	sh	w

WORD FAMILIES

The | _____ay | Family

Print the | ____ ay | words that you made.

1. _____   4. _____
2. _____   5. _____
3. _____   6. _____

Put a * beside your favorite | ____ay | word.

Print it in a sentence.

_____

_____

WORD FAMILIES

The | _____aw | Family

Print the | ____ aw | words that you made.

1. _____   4. _____
2. _____   5. _____
3. _____   6. _____

Put a * beside your favorite | ____aw | word.

Print it in a sentence.

_____

_____

Instructions: Mount on a sturdy backing and laminate. Cut out the puzzle pieces and store them in a labeled envelope. Sttudents will match the word family with the initial consonant, blend or digraph.

| ay | | d | m |
| pl | st | p | w |

| aw | | cl | dr |
| j | s | l | r |

WORD FAMILIES

The [____ore] Family

Print the [____ ore] words that you made.

1. _____   4. _____
2. _____   5. _____
3. _____   6. _____

Put a * beside your favorite [____ore] word.

Print it in a sentence.

_____

_____

WORD FAMILIES

The [____est] Family

Print the [____ est] words that you made.

1. _____   4. _____
2. _____   5. _____
3. _____   6. _____

Put a * beside your favorite [____est] word.

Print it in a sentence.

_____

_____

Instructions: Mount on a sturdy backing and laminate. Cut out the puzzle pieces and store them in a labeled envelope. Students will match the word family with the initial consonant, blend or digraph.

| ore | | c | m |
| st | sc | t | w |

| est | | b | n |
| ch | w | r | t |

WORD FAMILIES

The | _____ ell | Family

Print the | _____ ell | words that you made.

1. _____   4. _____
2. _____   5. _____
3. _____   6. _____

Put a * beside your favorite | _____ ell | word.
Print it in a sentence.

_____

_____

WORD FAMILIES

The | _____ ent | Family

Print the | _____ ent | words that you made.

1. _____   4. _____
2. _____   5. _____
3. _____   6. _____

Put a * beside your favorite | _____ ent | word.
Print it in a sentence.

_____

_____

Instructions: Mount on a sturdy backing and laminate. Cut out the puzzle pieces and store them in a labeled envelope. The students will match the word family with the initial consonant, blend or digraph.

ell		b	f
t	sm	w	y

ent		c	b
s	l	t	w

WORD FAMILIES

The | _____eam | Family

Print the | ____ eam | words that you made.

1. _____   4._____
2. _____   5._____
3. _____   6._____

Put a * beside your favorite | ___ eam | word.

Print it in a sentence.

_____

_____

WORD FAMILIES

The | _____ear | Family

Print the | ____ ear | words that you made.

1. _____   4._____
2. _____   5._____
3. _____   6._____

Put a * beside your favorite | ____ ear | word.

Print it in a sentence.

_____

_____

Instructions: Mount on a sturdy backing and laminate. Cut out the puzzle pieces and store them in a labeled evelope. The students will match the word family with the initial consonant, blend or digraph.

eam		t	cr
dr	st	s	cs

ear		b	f
t	h	n	y

WORD FAMILIES

The | _____eat | Family

Print the | ____ eat | words that you made.

1. _____   4. _____

2. _____   5. _____

3. _____   6. _____

Put a * beside your favorite | ___ eat | word.

Print it in a sentence.

_____

_____

WORD FAMILIES

The | _____ew | Family

Print the | ____ew | words that you made.

1. _____   4. _____

2. _____   5. _____

3. _____   6. _____

Put a * beside your favorite | ___ ew | word.

Print it in a sentence.

_____

_____

Instructions: Mount on a sturdy backing and laminate. Cut out the puzzle pieces and store them in a labeled envelope. Students will match the word family with the initial consonant, blend or digraph.

eat	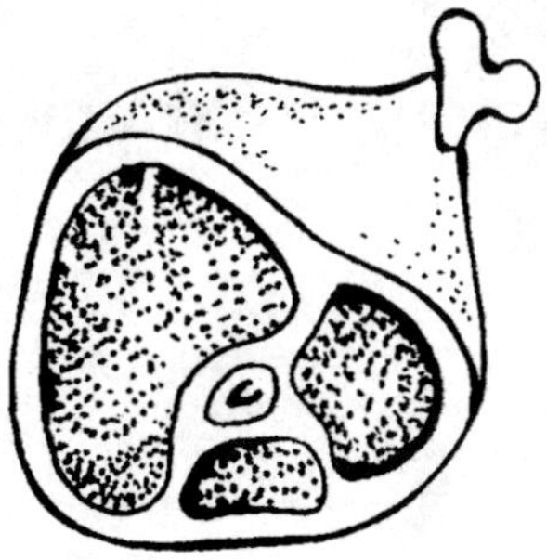	b	n
h	s	tr	m

ew		ch	f
gr	bl	kn	n

WORD FAMILIES

The [____eak] Family

Print the [___ eak] words that you made.

1. _____   4. _____

2. _____   5. _____

3. _____   6. _____

Put a * beside your favorite [___ eak] word.

Print it in a sentence.

_____

_____

WORD FAMILIES

The [____ue] Family

Print the [____ ue] words that you made.

1. _____   4. _____

2. _____   5. _____

3. _____   6. _____

Put a * beside your favorite [___ ue] word.

Print it in a sentence.

_____

_____

Instructions: Mount on a sturdy backing and laminate. Cut out the puzzle pieces and store them in a labeled envelope. The students will match the word family with the initial consonant, blend or digraph.

eak		b	cr
sn	sp	l	w

ue		bl	d
cl	gl	tr	fl

WORD FAMILIES

The | ____eed | Family

Print the | ____ eed | words that you made.

1. _____   4. _____
2. _____   5. _____
3. _____   6. _____

Put a * beside your favorite | ___ eed | word.

Print it in a sentence.

_____

_____

WORD FAMILIES

The | ____eet | Family

Print the | ____ eet | words that you made.

1. _____   4. _____
2. _____   5. _____
3. _____   6. _____

Put a * beside your favorite | ___ eet | word.

Print it in a sentence.

_____

_____

Instructions: Mount on a sturdy backing and laminate. Cut out the puzzle pieces and store them in a labeled envelope. Students will match the word family with the initial consonant, blend or digraph.

eed		**f**	**n**
s	**sp**	**w**	**gr**

eet		**f**	**m**
sh	**sw**	**gr**	**str**

WORD FAMILIES

The | ____eep | Family

Print the | ____ eep | words that you made.

1. _____   4. _____
2. _____   5. _____
3. _____   6. _____

Put a * beside your favorite | ___ eep | word.

Print it in a sentence.

_____

_____

WORD FAMILIES

The | ____ide | Family

Print the | ____ ide | words that you made.

1. _____   4. _____
2. _____   5. _____
3. _____   6. _____

Put a * beside your favorite | ___ ide | word.

Print it in a sentence.

_____

_____

Instructions: Mount on a sturdy backing and laminate. Cut out the puzzle pieces and store them in a labeled envelope. The students will match the word family with the initial consonant, blend or digraph.

eep		d	cr
k	sh	sl	st

ide		h	br
r	s	w	sl

WORD FAMILIES

The | ____ice | Family

Print the | ___ ice | words that you made.

1. _____   4. _____

2. _____   5. _____

3. _____   6. _____

Put a * beside your favorite | ___ ice | word.

Print it in a sentence.

_____

_____

WORD FAMILIES

The | ____ill | Family

Print the | ____ ill | words that you made.

1. _____   4. _____

2. _____   5. _____

3. _____   6. _____

Put a * beside your favorite | ___ ill | word.

Print it in a sentence.

_____

_____

Instructions: Mount on a sturdy backing and laminate. Cut out the puzzle pieces and store them in a labeled envelope. Students will match the word family with the initial consonant, blend or digraph

ice		n	m
pr	r	sl	sp

ill		f	b
h	p	w	k

WORD FAMILIES

The | _____ight | Family

Print the | ____ ight | words that you made.

1. _____   4. _____
2. _____   5. _____
3. _____   6. _____

Put a * beside your favorite | ___ ight | word.

Print it in a sentence.

_____

_____

WORD FAMILIES

The | _____ind | Family

Print the | ____ ind | words that you made.

1. _____   4. _____
2. _____   5. _____
3. _____   6. _____

Put a * beside your favorite | ___ ind | word.

Print it in a sentence.

_____

_____

Instructions: Mount on a sturdy backing and laminate. Cut out the puzzle pieces and store them in a labeled envelope. Students will match the word family with the initial consonant, blend or digraph.

ight		f	l
m	r	s	n

ind		f	m
k	bl	w	

WORD FAMILIES

The [_____ing] Family

Print the [_____ ing] words that you made.

1. _____   4. _____

2. _____   5. _____

3. _____   6. _____

Put a * beside your favorite [___ ing] word.

Print it in a sentence.

_____

_____

WORD FAMILIES

The [_____ine] Family

Print the [_____ ine] words that you made.

1. _____   4. _____

2. _____   5. _____

3. _____   6. _____

Put a * beside your favorite [___ ine] word.

Print it in a sentence.

_____

_____

Instructions: Mount on a sturdy backing and laminate. Cut out the puzzle pieces and store them in a labeled envelope. Students will match the word family with the initial consonant, blend or digraph.

| ing | | br | k |
| r | s | th | sw |

| ine | | f | l |
| p | m | n | sh |

WORD FAMILIES

The [____ink] Family

Print the [____ ink] words that you made.

1. _____   4. _____
2. _____   5. _____
3. _____   6. _____

Put a * beside your favorite [___ ink] word.

Print it in a sentence.

_____

_____

WORD FAMILIES

The [____ick] Family

Print the [____ ick] words that you made.

1. _____   4. _____
2. _____   5. _____
3. _____   6. _____

Put a * beside your favorite [___ ick] word.

Print it in a sentence.

_____

_____

Instructions: Mount on a sturdy backing and laminate. Cut out the puzzle pieces and store them in a labeled envelope. The students will match the word family with the initial consonant, blend or digraph

ink		dr	p
s	th	w	st

ick		br	k
p	s	st	tr

© On The Mark Press • S&S Learning Materials

OTM-1807 • SSR1-07 Building Word Families #2

WORD FAMILIES

The | ____ook | Family

Print the | ____ ook | words that you made.

1. _____   4. _____
2. _____   5. _____
3. _____   6. _____

Put a * beside your favorite | ___ ook | word.

Print it in a sentence.

_____

_____

WORD FAMILIES

The | ____ock | Family

Print the | ____ ock | words that you made.

1. _____   4. _____
2. _____   5. _____
3. _____   6. _____

Put a * beside your favorite | ___ ock | word.

Print it in a sentence.

_____

_____

Instructions: Mount on a sturdy backing and laminate. Cut out the puzzle pieces and store them in a labeled envelope. The students will match the word family with the initial consonant, blend or digraph.

ook		b	c
h	l	t	sh

ock		bl	cl
d	l	s	sh

WORD FAMILIES

The [____oke] Family

Print the [____ oke] words that you made.

1. _____   4._____
2. _____   5._____
3. _____   6._____

Put a * beside your favorite [___ oke] word.

Print it in a sentence.

_____

_____

WORD FAMILIES

The [____ose] Family

Print the [____ ose] words that you made.

1. _____   4._____
2. _____   5._____
3. _____   6._____

Put a * beside your favorite [___ ose] word.

Print it in a sentence.

_____

_____

Instructions: Mount on a sturdy backing and laminate. Cut out the puzzle pieces and store them in a labeled envelope. The students will match the word family with the initial consonant, blend or digraph.

oke		br	c
j	p	w	sm

ose		ch	cl
h	n	r	th

WORD FAMILIES

The | ____oat | Family

Print the | ____ oat | words that you made.

1. _____   4. _____
2. _____   5. _____
3. _____   6. _____

Put a * beside your favorite | ___ oat | word.

Print it in a sentence.

_____

_____

WORD FAMILIES

The | ____old | Family

Print the | ____ old | words that you made.

1. _____   4. _____
2. _____   5. _____
3. _____   6. _____

Put a * beside your favorite | ___ old | word.

Print it in a sentence.

_____

_____

Instructions: Mount on a sturdy backing and laminate. Cut out the puzzle pieces and store them in a labeled envelope. The students will match the word family with the initial consonant, blend or digraph.

oat		b	c
fl	g	thr	m
old		c	g
h	f	s	t

WORD FAMILIES

The [____ound] Family

Print the [____ ound] words that you made.

1. _____   4. _____
2. _____   5. _____
3. _____   6. _____

Put a * beside your favorite [___ ound] word.
  Print it in a sentence.

_____

_____

WORD FAMILIES

The [____ow] Family

Print the [____ ow] words that you made.

1. _____   4. _____
2. _____   5. _____
3. _____   6. _____

Put a * beside your favorite [___ ow] word.
Print it in a sentence.

_____

_____

Instructions: Mount on a sturdy backing and laminate. Cut out the puzzle pieces and store them in a labeled envelope. The students will match the word family with the initial consonant, blend or digraph.

ound		f	h
gr	r	s	p
ow		b	bl
gr	kn	sh	sn

WORD FAMILIES

The [____ow] Family

Print the [____ ow] words that you made.

1. _____ 4. _____
2. _____ 5. _____
3. _____ 6. _____

Put a * beside your favorite [___ ow] word.

Print it in a sentence.

_____

_____

WORD FAMILIES

The [_____] Family

Print the [____] words that you made.

1. _____ 4. _____
2. _____ 5. _____
3. _____ 6. _____

Put a * beside your favorite [___] word.

Print it in a sentence.

_____

_____

Instructions: Mount on a sturdy backing and laminate. Cut out the puzzle pieces and store them in a labeled envelope. Students will match the word family with the initial consonant, blend or digraph.

ow		c	h
n	w	s	pl

OW

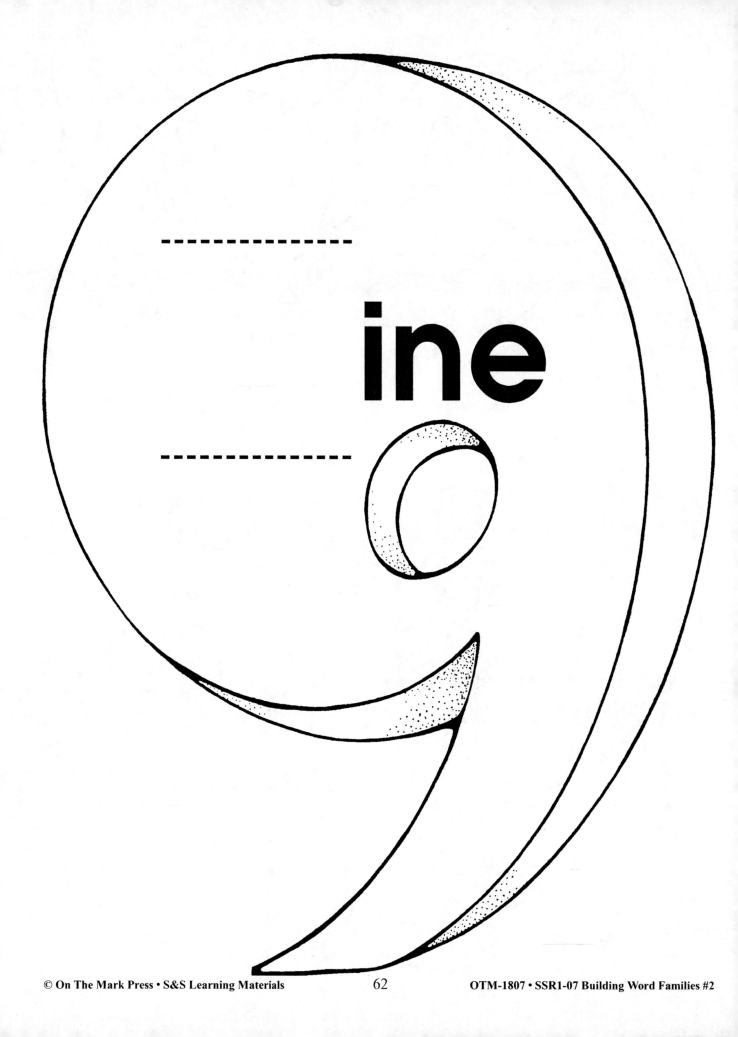

ine

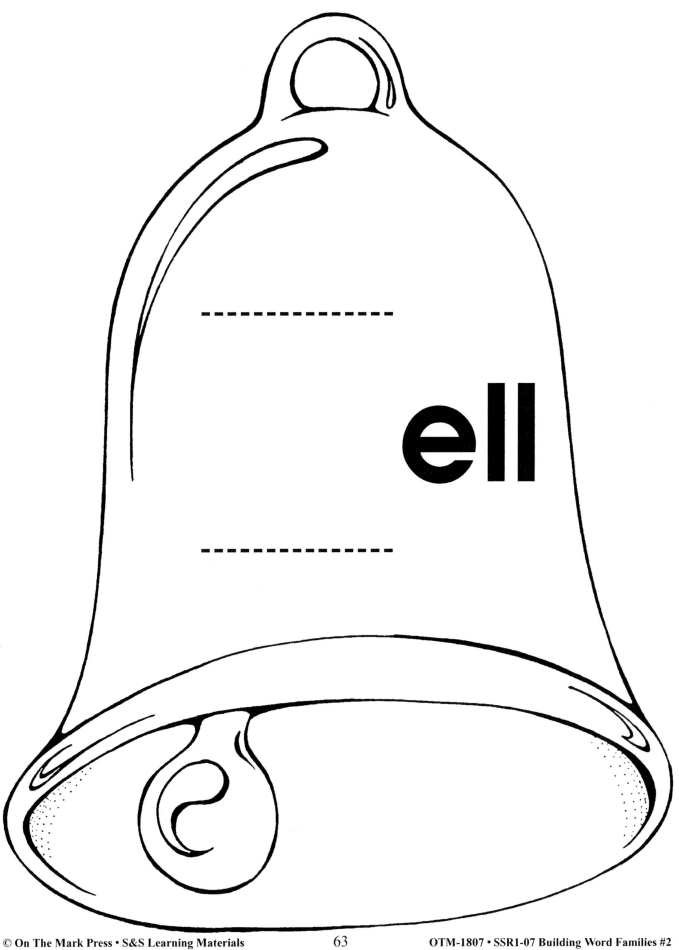

ell

_____ ing

_____

OTM-1807 • SSR1-07 Building Word Families #2

- - - - - - - - - - - - - -

ook

- - - - - - - - - - - - - -

----

ent

ail

----

ake

Word Family Review

Word List

wade	name	bake
came	fade	game
cake	take	made
make	trade	same

Write each word under the correct word family.

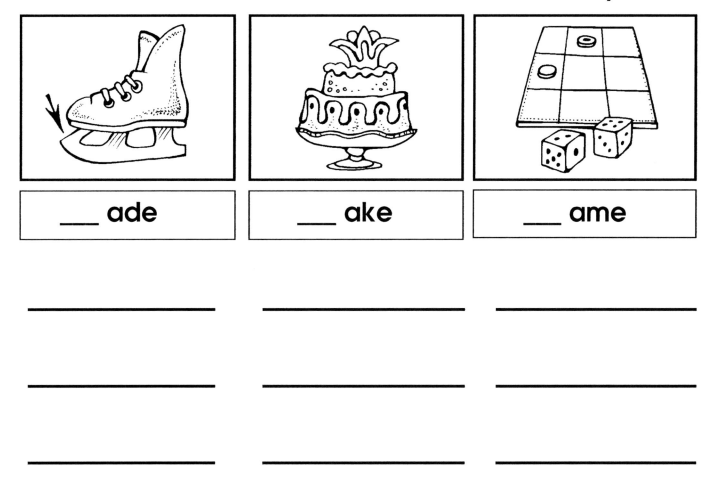

___ ade	___ ake	___ ame

_____ _____ _____

_____ _____ _____

_____ _____ _____

_____ _____ _____

Word Family Review

Word List

part	gave	date
gate	late	wave
save	smart	plate
start	brave	chart

Write each word under the correct word family

__ art

__ ate

__ ave

_____   _____   _____

_____   _____   _____

_____   _____   _____

_____   _____   _____

Word Family Review

Word List

mail	train	stay
rain	play	trail
day	sail	plain
tail	main	way

Write each word under the correct word family.

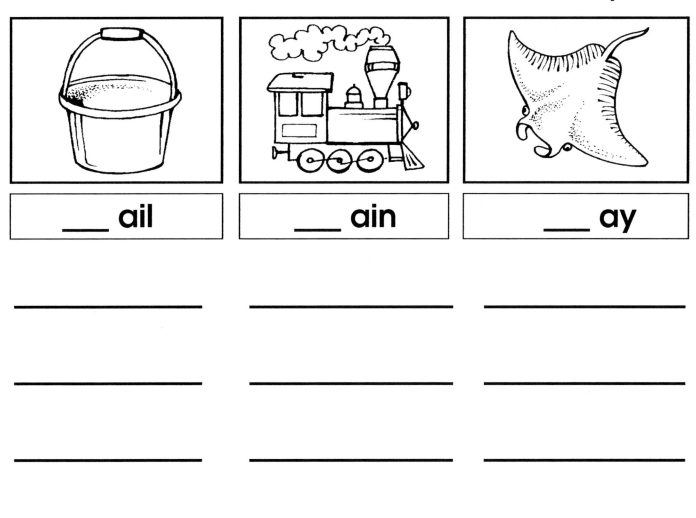

___ ail	___ ain	___ ay

_____   _____   _____

_____   _____   _____

_____   _____   _____

_____   _____   _____

Word Family Review

Word List

back	thank	small
ball	black	blank
bank	call	snack
sack	sank	fall

Write each word under the correct word family.

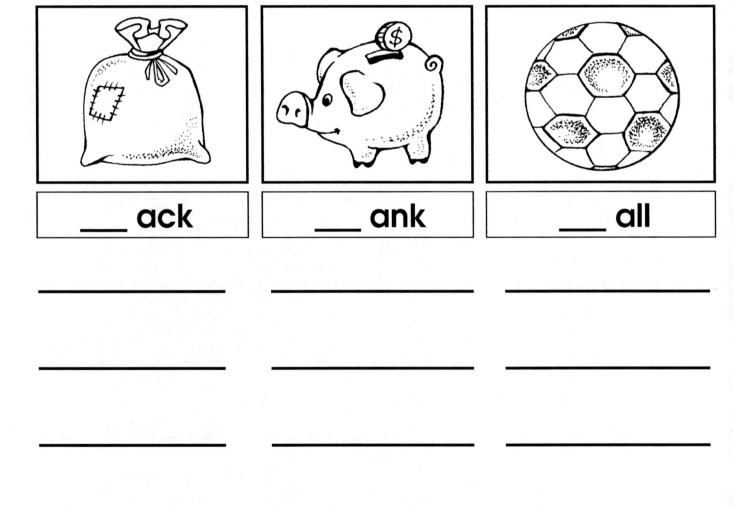

__ ack	__ ank	__ all

_____   _____   _____

_____   _____   _____

_____   _____   _____

_____   _____   _____

Word Family Review

Word List

saw	store
more	claw
draw	tore
wore	law

Write each word under the correct word family.

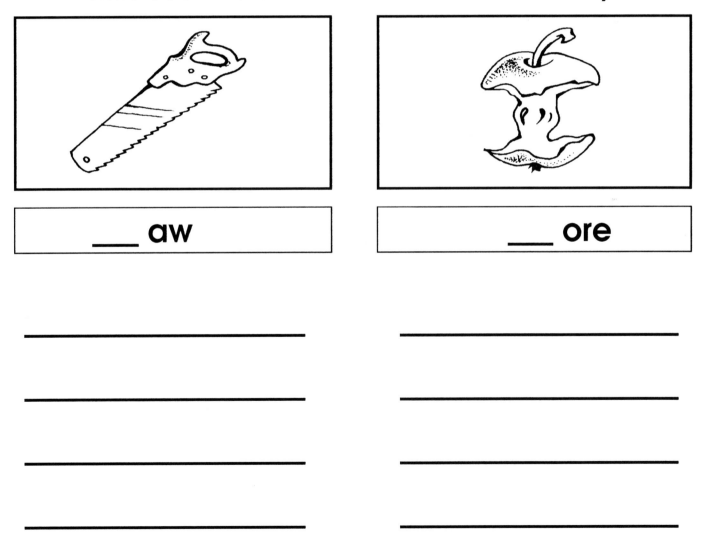

__ aw

__ ore

_____

_____

_____

_____

Word Family Review

Word List

keep	meet	speed
need	deep	sheet
feet	feed	sleep
sheep	sweet	seed

Write each word under the correct word family.

  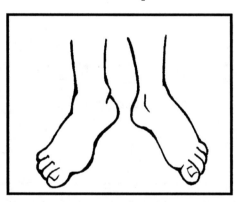

___eep	___eed	___eet

Word Family Review

Word List

team	sneak	heat
seat	cream	speak
weak	neat	steam
dream	leak	treat

Write each word under the correct word family.

 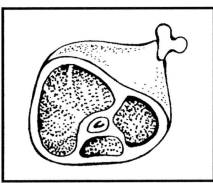 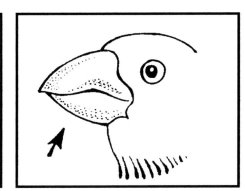

___ eam	___ eat	___ eak

_____   _____   _____

_____   _____   _____

_____   _____   _____

_____   _____   _____

Word Family Review

Word List

best	well	went
fell	tent	test
sent	nest	smell
rest	tell	lent

Write each word under the correct word family.

 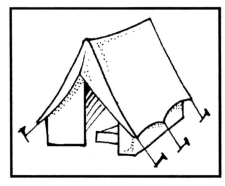 

___ ell	___ ent	___ est
_____	_____	_____
_____	_____	_____
_____	_____	_____
_____	_____	_____

Word Family Review

Word List

bear	hair
pair	near
hear	chair
wear	fair

Write each word under the correct word family.

_____ ear

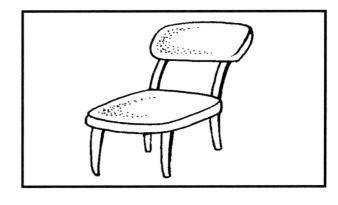

_____ air

_____

_____

_____

_____

_____

_____

_____

_____

Word Family Review

Word List

new	true
blue	few
chew	due
glue	grew

Write each word under the correct word family.

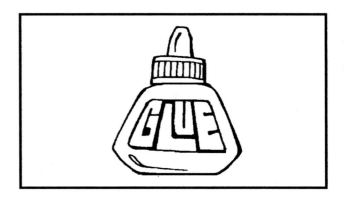

___ ew

___ ue

_____

_____

_____

_____

_____

_____

Word Family Review

Word List

nice	nine	wide
hide	price	shine
fine	ride	slice
mice	mine	slide

Write each word under the correct word family.

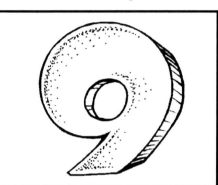

___ ice	___ ide	___ ine

_____ _____ _____

_____ _____ _____

_____ _____ _____

_____ _____ _____

Word Family Review

Word List

fill	find	swing
kind	bring	bill
thing	hill	blind
will	mind	sing

Write each word under the correct word family.

  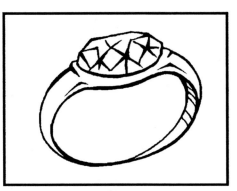

___ ill	___ ind	___ ing
_____	_____	_____
_____	_____	_____
_____	_____	_____
_____	_____	_____

Word Family Review

Word List

brick	think	might
drink	night	trick
light	sick	pink
pick	sink	right

Write each list word under the right heading.

___ ick	___ ink	___ ight

_____ _____ _____

_____ _____ _____

_____ _____ _____

_____ _____ _____

Word Family Review

Word List

sock	cold	took
hold	look	clock
book	lock	sold
block	told	cook

Write each word under the correct word family.

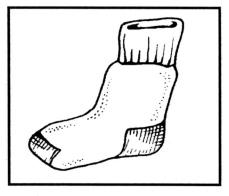

___ ock	___ old	___ ook

_____   _____   _____

_____   _____   _____

_____   _____   _____

_____   _____   _____

Word Family Review

Word List

boat	nose	woke
rose	broke	float
joke	goat	those
coat	chose	smoke

Write each word under the correct word family.

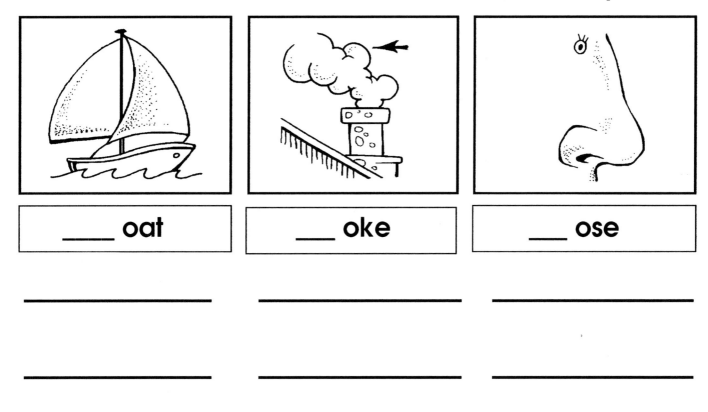

___ oat	___ oke	___ ose

_____ _____ _____

_____ _____ _____

_____ _____ _____

_____ _____ _____

Word Family Review

Word List

snow	now	sound
cow	found	plow
round	grow	know
show	how	ground

Write each list word under the right heading.

___ ow	___ ow	___ ound
as in snow	as in cow	as in sound

_____   _____   _____

_____   _____   _____

_____   _____   _____

_____   _____   _____

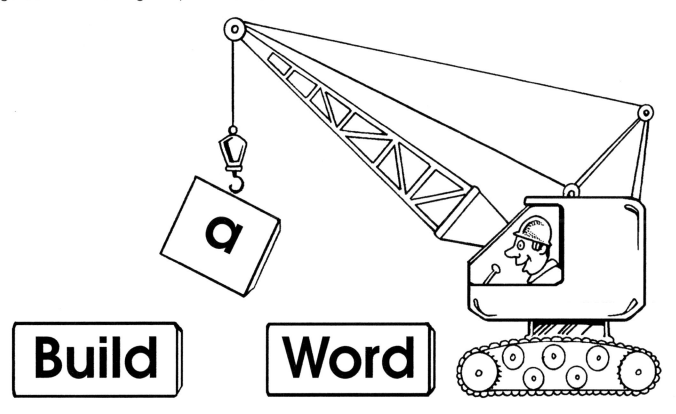

- Say the name of the Word Family.

- Match it to make a new word.

- What word have you made?

  - Can you say it slowly?

  - Can you say it fast?

Instructions: Mount on a sturdy backing and laminate. Cut out the cards and store them in an envelope. The students will use the word cards in sorting activities and games.

Instructions: Mount on a sturdy backing and laminate. Cut out and attach the stops to each end of the letter strip once inserted in the slide.

__ ow	__ ine	__ ell
n	f	b
h	l	f
s	p	t
br	m	y
pl	n	w
	sh	sm

__ ing	__ook	__ ent
br	b	b
k	c	s
r	h	t
s	l	w
th	t	l
sw	sh	c

Instructions: Mount on a sturdy backing and laminate. Cut out and attach the stops to each end of the letter strip once inserted in the slide card.

__ail	__ake
m	b
n	c
p	l
s	t
t	r
tr	br

Instructions: Mount on a sturdy backing and laminate. Cut out and attach the stops to each end of the letter strip once inserted in the slide card.

STOP	STOP
STOP	STOP
STOP	STOP
STOP	STOP
STOP	STOP
STOP	STOP
STOP	STOP

Instructions: Mount on a sturdy backing and laminate. Attach the labels to envelopes and use them to store the appropriate word family cards.

__ade

__ake

__ame

__art

__ate

__ave

__ail

__ain

Instructions: Mount on a sturdy backing and laminate. Attach the labels to envelopes and use them to store the appropriate word family cards.

__ay

__ack

__ank

__all

__aw

__ore

__eep

__eed

Instructions: Mount on a sturdy backing and laminate. Attach the labels to envelopes and use them to store the appropriate word family cards.

_eet

_eam

_eat

_eak

_ell

_ent

_est

_ear

Instructions: Mount on a sturdy backing and laminate. Attach the labels to envelopes and use them to store the appropriate word family cards.

_air

_ew

_ue

_ice

_ide

_ine

_ill

_ind

Instructions: Mount on a sturdy backing and laminate. Attach the labels to envelopes and use them to store the appropriate word family cards.

_ing

_ick

_ink

_ight

_ock

_old

_ook

_oat

Instructions: Mount on a sturdy backing and laminate. Attach the labels to envelopes and use them to store the appropriate word family cards.

_ _oke

_ _ose

_ _ow

_ _ow

_ _ound

Publication Listing

Code #	Title and Grade
SSC1-12	A Time of Plenty Gr. 2
SSN1-92	Abel's Island NS Gr. 4-6
SSF1-16	Aboriginal Peoples of Canada Gr. 7-8
SSK1-31	Addition & Subtraction Drills Gr. 1-3
SSK1-28	Addition Drills Gr. 1-3
SSY1-04	Addition Gr. 1-3
SSN1-174	Adv. of Huckle Berry Finn NS Gr. 7-8
SSB1-63	African Animals Gr 4-6
SSB1-29	All About Bears Gr. 1-2
SSF1-08	All About Boats Gr. 2-3
SSJ1-02	All About Canada Gr. 2
SSB1-54	All About Cattle Gr. 4-6
SSN1-10	All About Colours Gr. P-1
SSB1-93	All About Dinosaurs Gr. 2
SSN1-14	All About Dragons Gr. 3-5
SSB1-07	All About Elephants Gr. 3-4
SSB1-68	All About Fish Gr. 4-6
SSN1-39	All About Giants Gr. 2-3
SSH1-15	All About Jobs Gr. 1-3
SSH1-05	All About Me Gr. 1
SSA1-02	All About Mexico Gr. 4-6
SSR1-28	All About Nouns Gr. 5-7
SSF1-09	All About Planes Gr. 2-3
SSB1-33	All About Plants Gr. 2-3
SSR1-29	All About Pronouns Gr. 5-7
SSB1-12	All About Rabbits Gr. 2-3
SSB1-58	All About Spiders Gr. 4-6
SSA1-03	All About the Desert Gr. 4-6
SSA1-04	All About the Ocean Gr. 5-7
SSZ1-01	All About the Olympics Gr. 2-4
SSB1-49	All About the Sea Gr. 4-6
SSK1-06	All About Time Gr. 4-6
SSF1-07	All About Trains Gr. 2-3
SSH1-18	All About Transportation Gr. 2
SSB1-01	All About Trees Gr. 4-6
SSB1-61	All About Weather Gr. 7-8
SSB1-06	All About Whales Gr. 3-4
SSPC-26	All Kinds of Clocks B/W Pictures
SSB1-110	All Kinds of Structures Gr. 1
SSH1-19	All Kinds of Vehicles Gr. 3
SSF1-01	Amazing Aztecs Gr. 4-6
SSB1-92	Amazing Earthworms Gr. 2-3
SSJ1-50	Amazing Facts in Cdn History Gr. 4-6
SSB1-32	Amazing Insects Gr. 4-6
SSN1-132	Amelia Bedelia–Camping NS 1-3
SSN1-68	Amelia Bedelia NS 1-3
SSN1-155	Amelia Bedelia-Surprise Shower NS 1-3
SSA1-13	America The Beautiful Gr. 4-6
SSN1-57	Amish Adventure NS 7-8
SSF1-02	Ancient China Gr. 4-6
SSF1-18	Ancient Egypt Gr. 4-6
SSF1-21	Ancient Greece Gr. 4-6
SSF1-19	Ancient Rome Gr. 4-6
SSQ1-06	Animal Town – Big Book Pkg 1-3
SSQ1-02	Animals Prepare Winter – Big Book Pkg 1-3
SSN1-150	Animorphs the Invasion NS 4-6
SSN1-53	Anne of Green Gables NS 7-8
SSB1-40	Apple Celebration Gr. 4-6
SSB1-04	Apple Mania Gr. 2-3
SSB1-38	Apples are the Greatest Gr. P-K
SSB1-59	Arctic Animals Gr. 4-6
SSN1-162	Arnold Lobel Author Study Gr. 2-3
SSPC-22	Australia B/W Pictures
SSA1-05	Australia Gr. 5-8
SSM1-03	Autumn in the Woodlot Gr. 2-3
SSM1-08	Autumn Wonders Gr. 1
SSN1-41	Baby Sister for Frances NS 1-3
SSPC-19	Back to School B/W Pictures
SSC1-33	Back to School Gr. 2-3
SSN1-224	Banner in the Sky NS 7-8
SSN1-36	Bargain for Frances NS 1-3
SSB1-82	Bats Gr. 4-6
SSN1-71	BB – Drug Free Zone NS Gr. 1-3
SSN1-88	BB – In the Freaky House NS 1-3
SSN1-78	BB – Media Madness NS 1-3
SSN1-69	BB – Wheelchair Commando NS 1-3
SSN1-119	Be a Perfect Person-3 Days NS 4-6
SSC1-15	Be My Valentine Gr. 1
SSD1-01	Be Safe Not Sorry Gr. P-1
SSN1-09	Bear Tales Gr. 2-4
SSB1-28	Bears Gr. 4-6
SSN1-202	Bears in Literature Gr. 1-3
SSN1-40	Beatrix Potter Gr. 2-4
SSN1-129	Beatrix Potter: Activity Biography Gr. 2-4
SSB1-47	Beautiful Bugs Gr. 1
SSB1-21	Beavers Gr. 3-5
SSN1-257	Because of Winn-Dixie NS Gr. 4-6
SSR1-53	Beginning Manuscript Gr. Pk-2
SSR1-54	Beginning Cursive Gr. 2-4
SSR1-57	Beginning and Practice Manuscript Gr. PK-2
SSR1-58	Beginning and Practice Cursive Gr. 2-4
SSN1-33	Bedtime for Frances NS 1-3
SSN1-114	Best Christmas Pageant Ever NS Gr. 4-6
SSN1-32	Best Friends for Frances NS Gr. 1-3
SSB1-39	Best Friends Pets Gr. P-K
SSN1-185	BFG NS Gr. 4-6
SSJ1-61	Big Book of Canadian Celebrations Gr. 1-3
SSJ1-62	Big Book of Canadian Celebrations Gr. 4-6
SSN1-35	Birthday for Frances NS Gr. 1-3
SSN1-107	Borrowers NS Gr. 4-6
SSC1-16	Bouquet of Valentines Gr. 2
SSN1-29	Bread & Jam for Frances NS Gr. 1-3
SSN1-63	Bridge to Terabithia NS Gr. 4-6
SSY1-24	BTS Numeración Gr. 1-3
SSY1-25	BTS Adición Gr. 1-3
SSY1-26	BTS Sustracción Gr. 1-3
SSY1-27	BTS Fonética Gr. 1-3
SSY1-28	BTS Leer para Entender Gr. 1-3
SSY1-29	BTS Uso de las Mayúsculas y Reglas de Puntuación Gr. 1-3
SSY1-30	BTS Composición de Oraciones Gr. 1-3
SSY1-31	BTS Composici13n de Historias Gr. 1-3
SSN1-256	Bud, Not Buddy NS Gr. 4-6
SSB1-31	Bugs, Bugs & More Bugs Gr. 2-3
SSR1-07	Building Word Families L.V. Gr. 1-2
SSR1-05	Building Word Families S.V. Gr. 1-2
SSN1-204	Bunnicula NS Gr. 4-6
SSB1-80	Butterflies & Caterpillars Gr. 1-2
SSN1-164	Call It Courage NS Gr. 7-8
SSN1-67	Call of the Wild NS Gr. 7-8
SSJ1-41	Canada & It's Trading Partners 6-8
SSPC-28	Canada B/W Pictures
SSN1-173	Canada Geese Quilt NS Gr. 4-6
SSJ1-01	Canada Gr. 1
SSJ1-33	Canada's Capital Cities Gr. 4-6
SSJ1-43	Canada's Confederation Gr. 7-8
SSF1-04	Canada's First Nations Gr. 7-8
SSJ1-51	Canada's Landmarks Gr. 1-3
SSJ1-48	Canada's Landmarks Gr. 4-6
SSJ1-60	Canada's Links to the World Gr. 5-8
SSJ1-42	Canada's Traditions & Celeb. Gr. 1-3
SSB1-45	Canadian Animals Gr. 1-2
SSJ1-37	Canadian Arctic Inuit Gr. 2-3
SSJ1-53	Canadian Black History Gr. 4-8
SSJ1-57	Canadian Comprehension Gr. 1-2
SSJ1-58	Canadian Comprehension Gr. 3-4
SSJ1-59	Canadian Comprehension Gr. 5-6
SSJ1-46	Canadian Industries Gr. 4-6
SSK1-12	Canadian Problem Solving Gr. 4-6
SSJ1-38	Canadian Provinces & Terr. Gr. 4-6
SSY1-07	Capitalization & Punctuation Gr. 1-3
SSN1-198	Captain Courageous NS Gr. 7-8
SSK1-11	Cars Problem Solving Gr. 3-4
SSN1-154	Castle in the Attic NS Gr. 4-6
SSF1-31	Castles & Kings Gr. 4-6
SSN1-144	Cat Ate My Gymsuit NS Gr. 4-6
SSPC-38	Cats B/W Pictures
SSB1-50	Cats – Domestic & Wild Gr. 4-6
SSN1-34	Cats in Literature Gr. 3-6
SSN1-212	Cay NS Gr. 7-8
SSM1-09	Celebrate Autumn Gr. 4-6
SSC1-39	Celebrate Christmas Gr. 4-6
SSC1-31	Celebrate Easter Gr. 4-6
SSC1-23	Celebrate Shamrock Day Gr. 2
SSM1-11	Celebrate Spring Gr. 4-6
SSC1-13	Celebrate Thanksgiving R. 3-4
SSM1-06	Celebrate Winter Gr. 4-6
SSB1-107	Cells, Tissues & Organs Gr. 7-8
SSB1-101	Characteristics of Flight Gr. 4-6
SSN1-66	Charlie & Chocolate Factory NS Gr. 4-6
SSN1-23	Charlotte's Web NS Gr. 4-6
SSB1-37	Chicks N'Ducks Gr. 2-4
SSA1-09	China Today Gr. 5-8
SSN1-70	Chocolate Fever NS Gr. 4-6
SSN1-241	Chocolate Touch NS Gr. 4-6
SSC1-38	Christmas Around the World Gr. 4-6
SSPC-42	Christmas B/W Pictures
SST1-08A	Christmas Gr. JK/SK
SST1-08B	Christmas Gr. 1
SST1-08C	Christmas Gr. 2-3
SSC1-04	Christmas Magic Gr. 1
SSC1-03	Christmas Tales Gr. 2-3
SSG1-06	Cinematography Gr. 5-8
SSPC-13	Circus B/W Pictures
SSF1-03	Circus Magic Gr. 3-4
SSJ1-52	Citizenship/Immigration Gr. 4-8
SSN1-104	Classical Poetry Gr. 7-12
SSN1-227	Color Gr. 1-3
SSN1-203	Colour Gr. 1-3
SSN1-135	Come Back Amelia Bedelia NS 1-3
SSH1-11	Community Helpers Gr. 1-3
SSK1-02	Concept Cards & Activities Gr. P-1
SSN1-183	Copper Sunrise NS Gr. 7-8
SSN1-86	Corduroy & Pocket Corduroy NS 1-3
SSN1-124	Could Dracula Live in Wood NS 4-6
SSN1-148	Cowboy's Don't Cry NS Gr. 7-8
SSR1-01	Creativity with Food Gr. 4-8
SSB1-34	Creatures of the Sea Gr. 2-4
SSN1-208	Curse of the Viking Grave NS 7-8
SSN1-134	Danny Champion of World NS 4-6
SSN1-98	Danny's Run NS Gr. 7-8
SSK1-21	Data Management Gr. 4-6
SSB1-53	Dealing with Dinosaurs Gr. 4-6
SSN1-178	Dear Mr. Henshaw NS Gr. 4-6
SSB1-22	Deer Gr. 3-5
SSPC-20	Desert B/W Pictures
SSJ1-40	Development of Western Canada 7-8
SSA1-16	Development of Manufacturing 7-9
SSN1-105	Dicken's Christmas NS Gr. 7-8
SSN1-62	Different Dragons NS Gr. 4-6
SSPC-21	Dinosaurs B/W Pictures
SSB1-16	Dinosaurs Gr. 1
SST1-02A	Dinosaurs Gr. JK/SK
SST1-02B	Dinosaurs Gr. 1
SST1-02 C	Dinosaurs Gr. 2-3
SSN1-175	Dinosaurs in Literature Gr. 1-3
SSJ1-26	Discover Nova Scotia Gr. 5-7
SSJ1-36	Discover Nunavut Territory Gr. 5-7
SSJ1-25	Discover Ontario Gr. 5-7
SSJ1-24	Discover PEI Gr. 5-7
SSJ1-22	Discover Québec Gr. 5-7
SSL1-01	Discovering the Library Gr. 2-3
SSB1-106	Diversity of Living Things Gr. 4-6
SSK1-27	Division Drills Gr. 4-6
SSB1-30	Dogs – Wild & Tame Gr. 4-6
SSPC-31	Dogs B/W Pictures
SSN1-196	Dog's Don't Tell Jokes NS Gr. 4-6
SSN1-182	Door in the Wall NS Gr. 4-6
SSB1-87	Down by the Sea Gr. 1-3
SSN1-189	Dr. Jeckyll & Mr. Hyde NS Gr. 4-6
SSG1-07	Dragon Trivia Gr. P-8
SSN1-102	Dragon's Egg NS Gr. 4-6
SSN1-16	Dragons in Literature Gr. 3-6
SSC1-06	Early Christmas Gr. 3-5
SSB1-109	Earth's Crust Gr. 6-8
SSC1-21	Easter Adventures Gr. 3-4
SSC1-17	Easter Delights Gr. P-K
SSC1-19	Easter Surprises Gr. 1
SSPC-12	Egypt B/W Pictures
SSN1-255	Egypt Game NS Gr. 4-6
SSF1-28	Egyptians Today & Yesterday Gr. 2-3
SSJ1-49	Elections in Canada Gr. 4-8
SSB1-108	Electricity Gr. 4-6
SSN1-02	Elves & the Shoemaker NS Gr. 1-3
SSH1-14	Emotions Gr. P-2
SSB1-85	Energy Gr. 4-6
SSN1-108	English Language Gr. 10-12
SSN1-156	Enjoying Eric Wilson Series Gr. 5-7
SSB1-64	Environment Gr. 4-6
SSR1-12	ESL Teaching Ideas Gr. K-8
SSN1-258	Esperanza Rising NS Gr. 4-6
SSR1-22	Exercises in Grammar Gr. 6
SSR1-23	Exercises in Grammar Gr. 7
SSR1-24	Exercises in Grammar Gr. 8
SSF1-20	Exploration Gr. 4-6
SSF1-15	Explorers & Mapmakers of Can. 7-8
SSJ1-54	Exploring Canada Gr. 1-3
SSJ1-56	Exploring Canada Gr. 1-6
SSJ1-55	Exploring Canada Gr. 4-6
SSH1-20	Exploring My School & Community 1
SSPC-39	Fables B/W Pictures
SSN1-15	Fables Gr. 4-6
SSN1-04	Fairy Tale Magic Gr. 3-5
SSPC-11	Fairy Tales B/W Pictures
SSN1-11	Fairy Tales Gr. 1-2
SSN1-199	Family Under the Bridge NS Gr. 4-6
SSPC-41	Famous Canadians B/W Pictures
SSJ1-12	Famous Canadians Gr. 4-8
SSN1-210	Fantastic Mr. Fox NS Gr. 4-6
SSB1-36	Fantastic Plants Gr. 4-6
SSPC-04	Farm Animals B/W Pictures
SSB1-15	Farm Animals Gr. 1-2
SST1-03A	Farm Gr. JK/SK
SST1-03B	Farm Gr. 1
SST1-03C	Farm Gr. 2-3
SSJ1-05	Farming Community Gr. 3-4
SSB1-44	Farmyard Friends Gr. P-K
SSJ1-45	Fathers of Confederation Gr. 4-8
SSB1-19	Feathered Friends Gr. 4-6
SST1-05A	February Gr. JK/SK
SST1-05B	February Gr. 1
SST1-05C	February Gr. 2-3
SSN1-03	Festival of Fairytales Gr. 3-5
SSC1-36	Festivals Around the World Gr. 2-3
SSN1-168	First 100 Sight Words Gr. 1
SSC1-32	First Days at School Gr. 1
SSJ1-06	Fishing Community Gr. 3-4
SSN1-170	Flowers for Algernon NS Gr. 7-8
SSN1-261	Flat Stanley NS Gr. 1-3
SSN1-128	Fly Away Home NS Gr. 4-6
SSD1-05	Food: Fact, Fun & Fiction Gr. 1-3
SSD1-06	Food: Nutrition & Invention Gr. 4-6
SSB1-118	Force and Motion Gr. 1-3
SSB1-119	Force and Motion Gr. 4-6
SSB1-25	Foxes Gr. 3-5
SSN1-263	Fractured Fairy Tales NS Gr. 1-3
SSN1-172	Freckle Juice NS Gr. 1-3
SSB1-43	Friendly Frogs Gr. 1
SSN1-260	Frindle NS Gr. 4-6
SSB1-89	Fruits & Seeds Gr. 4-6
SSN1-137	Fudge-a-Mania NS Gr. 4-6
SSB1-14	Fun on the Farm Gr. 3-4
SSR1-49	Fun with Phonics Gr. 1-3
SSPC-06	Garden Flowers B/W Pictures
SSK1-03	Geometric Shapes Gr. 2-5
SSC1-18	Get the Rabbit Habit Gr. 1-2
SSN1-209	Giver, The NS Gr. 7-8
SSN1-190	Go Jump in the Pool NS Gr. 4-6
SSG1-03	Goal Setting Gr. 6-8
SSG1-08	Gr. 3 Test – Parent Guide
SSG1-99	Gr. 3 Test – Teacher Guide
SSG1-09	Gr. 6 Language Test–Parent Guide
SSG1-97	Gr. 6 Language Test–Teacher Guide
SSG1-10	Gr. 6 Math Test – Parent Guide
SSG1-96	Gr. 6 Math Test – Teacher Guide
SSG1-98	Gr. 6 Math/Lang. Test–Teacher Guide
SSK1-14	Graph for all Seasons Gr. 1-3
SSN1-117	Great Brain NS Gr. 4-6
SSN1-90	Great Expectations NS Gr. 7-8
SSN1-169	Great Gilly Hopkins NS Gr. 4-6
SSN1-197	Great Science Fair Disaster NS Gr. 4-6
SSN1-138	Greek Mythology Gr. 7-8
SSN1-113	Green Gables Detectives NS 4-6
SSC1-26	Groundhog Celebration Gr. 2
SSC1-25	Groundhog Day Gr. 1
SSB1-113	Growth & Change in Animals Gr. 2-3
SSB1-114	Growth & Change in Plants Gr. 2-3
SSB1-48	Guinea Pigs & Friends Gr. 3-5
SSB1-104	Habitats Gr. 4-6
SSPC-18	Halloween B/W Pictures
SST1-04A	Halloween Gr. JK/SK
SST1-04B	Halloween Gr. 1
SST1-04C	Halloween Gr. 2-3
SSC1-10	Halloween Gr. 4-6
SSC1-08	Halloween Happiness Gr. 1
SSC1-29	Halloween Spirits Gr. P-K
SSY1-13	Handwriting Manuscript Gr 1-3
SSY1-14	Handwriting Cursive Gr. 1-3
SSC1-42	Happy Valentines Day Gr. 3
SSN1-205	Harper Moon NS Gr. 7-8
SSN1-123	Harriet the Spy NS Gr. 4-6
SSC1-11	Harvest Time Wonders Gr. 1
SSN1-136	Hatchet NS Gr. 7-8
SSC1-09	Haunting Halloween Gr. 2-3
SSN1-91	Hawk & Stretch NS Gr. 4-6
SSC1-30	Hearts & Flowers Gr. P-K
SSN1-22	Heidi NS Gr. 4-6
SSN1-120	Help I'm Trapped in My NS Gr. 4-6
SSN1-24	Henry & the Clubhouse NS Gr. 4-6
SSN1-184	Hobbit NS Gr. 7-8
SSN1-122	Hoboken Chicken Emerg. NS 4-6
SSN1-250	Holes NS Gr. 4-6
SSN1-116	How Can a Frozen Detective NS 4-6
SSN1-89	How Can I be a Detective if I NS 4-6
SSN1-96	How Come the Best Clues... NS 4-6

Publication Listing

Code #	Title and Grade
SSN1-27	Unicorns in Literature Gr. 3-5
SSJ1-44	Upper & Lower Canada Gr. 7-8
SSN1-192	Using Novels Canadian North Gr. 7-8
SSC1-14	Valentines Day Gr. 5-8
SSPC-45	Vegetables B/W Pictures
SSY1-01	Very Hungry Caterpillar NS 30/Pkg Gr. 1-3
SSF1-13	Victorian Era Gr. 7-8
SSC1-35	Victorian Christmas Gr. 5-8
SSF1-17	Viking Age Gr. 4-6
SSN1-206	War with Grandpa SN Gr. 4-6
SSB1-91	Water Gr. 2-4
SSN1-166	Watership Down NS Gr. 7-8
SSH1-16	Ways We Travel Gr. P-K
SSN1-101	Wayside Sch. Little Stranger NS Gr. 4-6
SSN1-76	Wayside Sch. is Falling Down NS 4-6
SSB1-60	Weather Gr. 4-6
SSN1-17	Wee Folk in Literature Gr. 3-5
SSPC-08	Weeds B/W Pictures
SSQ1-04	Welcome Back – Big Book Pkg 1-3
SSB1-73	Whale Preservation Gr. 5-8
SSH1-08	What is a Community? Gr. 2-4
SSH1-01	What is a Family? Gr. 2-3
SSH1-09	What is a School? Gr. 1-2
SSJ1-32	What is Canada? Gr. P-K
SSN1-79	What is RAD? Read & Discover 2-4
SSB1-62	What is the Weather Today? Gr. 2-4
SSN1-194	What's a Daring Detective NS 4-6
SSH1-10	What's My Number Gr. P-K
SSR1-02	What's the Scoop on Words Gr. 4-6
SSN1-73	Where the Red Fern Grows NS Gr. 7-8
SSN1-87	Where the Wild Things Are NS Gr. 1-3
SSN1-187	Whipping Boy NS Gr. 4-6
SSN1-226	Who is Frances Rain? NS Gr. 4-6
SSN1-74	Who's Got Gertie & How...? NS Gr. 4-6
SSN1-131	Why did the Underwear ... NS 4-6
SSC1-28	Why Wear a Poppy? Gr. 2-3
SSJ1-11	Wild Animals of Canada Gr. 2-3
SSPC-07	Wild Flowers B/W Pictures
SSB1-18	Winter Birds Gr. 2-3
SSZ1-03	Winter Olympics Gr. 4-6
SSM1-04	Winter Wonderland Gr. 1
SSC1-01	Witches Gr. 3-4
SSN1-213	Wolf Island NS Gr. 1-3
SSE1-09	Wolfgang Amadeus Mozart 6-9
SSB1-23	Wolves Gr. 3-5
SSC1-20	Wonders of Easter Gr. 2
SSY1-15	Word Families Gr. 1-3
SSR1-59	Word Families 2,3 Letter Words Gr. 1-3
SSR1-60	Word Families 3, 4 Letter Words Gr. 1-3
SSR1-61	Word Families 2, 3, 4 Letter Words Big Book Gr. 1-3
SSB1-35	World of Horses Gr. 4-6
SSB1-13	World of Pets Gr. 2-3
SSF1-26	World War II Gr. 7-8
SSN1-221	Wrinkle in Time NS Gr. 7-8
SSPC-02	Zoo Animals B/W Pictures
SSB1-08	Zoo Animals Gr. 1-2
SSB1-09	Zoo Celebration Gr. 3-4

Code #	Title and Grade

Code #	Title and Grade

Code #	Title and Grade